GW00857393

FROM THE

CELTS TO THE

CATHARS

TWO SHORT BOOKS IN ONE

by

Tracy Saunders

PRISCILLIAN PRESS

From the Celts to the Cathars
Formerly published as two separate Kindle Shorts:
Celtic Influences in the North of Spain
Priscillian, the Cathars, and Me

The author of this work has been asserted with the
Copyright and Patents Act of 1988

ISBN: 9798851883668

COPYRIGHT: Tracy Saunders
PRISCILLIAN PRESS
Muxia, A Coruña, Spain, 15124

Cover Photograph by the late Laurent Crassous

From the Celts to
the Cathars

Celtic Influences in the
North of Spain
And the Roots of Heresy

Priscillian, the Cathars,
and Me

Books by Tracy Saunders

Fiction:

Pilgrimage to Heresy

St James' Rooster

Wellspring

Non-Fiction

The Indalo Quest

Being and Paradox

Two Girls/Dos Niñas

They Think You Are Jesus

The Little Fox House Cookbook

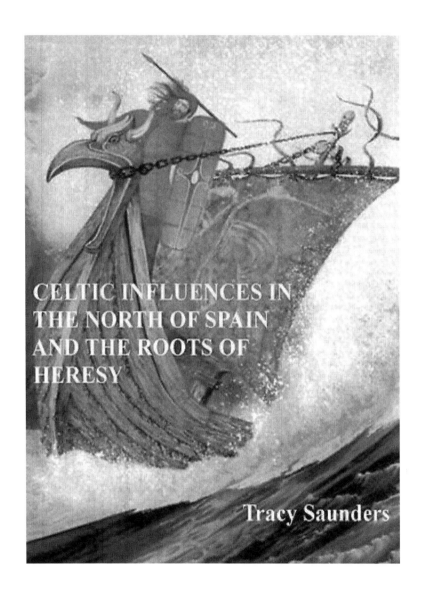

CELTIC INFLUENCES IN THE NORTH OF SPAIN AND THE ROOTS OF HERESY

Tracy Saunders

Celtic Influences in the North of Spain, and the Roots of Heresy

Tracy Saunders

The story of Spain begins somewhere in the confused muddle we call pre-history. Somewhere in the Peninsula, perhaps in the place we call Altamira, an artist picked up a piece of cold charcoal from the ashes of his campfire, and scratched a few lines on the wall of a cave. With a little practice, he produced a rough outline of a bird, a fish, a horse. He sat back, pleased with his work, and went to ask others to come and see what he had completed. The first art exhibition was a complete success.

As generations and aspiring artists perfected their techniques they began to experiment with other materials. Charcoal, they found, did not last, and so they replaced it with flint tools, and mixtures of ochre, blood, animal fat, plant extracts and minerals. Simultaneously, through the peninsula wherever there were caves, other works were in progress. In Altamira, the paintings are vivid and realistic: bison stand proudly: many of them painted on the cave's ceiling; horses gallop. In order to depict the muscles of these animals, the artists used the irregular relief of the rock's surface, and the colours are bold. Cave painting had been born, and with it, Art. More than 15,000 years ago, humankind learned to tell stories in pictorial form, and sometimes simply to dream.

 The end of the last Ice Age (about 8000BC) ushered in a long and transitional period before the arrival of the Neolithic cultures that came from the eastern Mediterranean five millennia later. We shall return to these people later, as they are the progenitors of our story.

As the climate began to warm, the nomadic life of the hunters and gatherers began to melt away northward with the icecaps as reindeer and other game left for cooler climates. In the next 50 or so centuries, new races began to enter the peninsula, most likely from North Africa. They were most likely proto-Berbers (the indigenous race of most of North West Africa today) and also Iberians, although as we shall see, these people came later and mixed with inhabitants. They brought their own form of art: rock shelter paintings which survive all along the eastern coast of Andalucía. For the first time, human figures begin to appear alongside the

 animals of the hunt. Stories were being told, but the quality was vastly inferior to those of earlier times: often just stick figures such as the famous "Índalo Man" of Almeria. *(See The Índalo Quest by Tracy Saunders)*

New influences seem to have reached the Peninsula by about 3000 BCE and began to spread slowly through the next couple of centuries. This culture seems to have come from the Eastern Mediterranean to present day Almeria where mineral deposits were found in plenty. Some of this new wave of people appear to have come directly by sea, possibly via Sicily; others from North Africa, possibly via the region which would later become Carthage. These people may have originated in the regions around Syria and preceded the Phoenicians in their voyages in search of metals. They were called the Hiberi, and again, we shall return to them later. Others likely came via the Danube Valley, but much later. The first split had begun.

Spreading eastward along what is now the Andalucian coastline, by the middle of the second millenium these people may well have founded the legendary civilization of Tartessos - known in the bible as Tarshish. It was likely in the south west of the peninsula in what stretches towards Cadíz from Huelva and into the area now occupied by Portugal.

The area was, and still is, rich in mineral deposits, especially copper and silver, and some tin and some gold. True Bronze Age technology began to emerge about this time.

Tartessos was long believed to have been a myth, another of the Atlantean-type until a German archaeologist named Adolf Schulten published a book on the subject in the 1920's. A major find appeared during routine dredging at the mouth of the Rio Tinto, near Huelva. (*Tinto* means "red", and the river runs with a clear copper colour. Smelting still takes place there.) An ancient wreck was found revealing more than 400 bronze weapons, needles, buttons and other artifacts.

Who were these people?

In order to investigate this thorny question, we have to go further into the mists of legend, and these are contradictory indeed.

The Irish Book of Leinster makes the extraordinary claim that the ancient peoples of Britain and Ireland were the descendants of some of the lost tribes of

Israel. They were, surprisingly described as fair-haired, with light eyes. These were the Hiberi, or Iberi, which at least one writer claims means Hebrew. This is the story of Fenius Farsaid, the leader of the Scythians - a region to the north east of the Black Sea bordering on the Russian steppes. Several comments on this story claim that Fenius was the descendant of Noah, via Japeth his son, and that he was active in helping to build the Tower of Babel. The story says that these people left their homeland and wandered to Egypt where they were welcomed by Pharaoh who wanted to learn their language. The son of their leader, whose name was Niul, fell in love with and married Pharaoh's daughter. Her name was Scota. They had a son named Gaedel Glas, sometimes spelled as Goedel. The generations pass, and a great grandson known as Eber Scot, was suspected of having plans to take over Egypt and his people are ejected from that land. They return to Scythia where, it is said, they dwelt in their boats in the marshes.

One day, a holy man, called in the story "a Druid", told them that he had had a vision of a land which he

called Irland. He prophesised: "Your people will not rest until they reach this land." Upon reaching the Danube, some of the Scythians decided to follow it, spreading their peoples upon the European lands as they wandered ever westwards. Unfortunately, since neither GPS nor Rand McNally had been invented in those days, the rest went a little off course and ended back in North Africa, likely in the regions of Libya, Tunisia (present day Carthage), or Algeria, where they supposedly stayed for 7 generations, which begs the question as to whether the druid, whose name was Caicher, described the topography of Irland to them very well. But I suppose even Druids make mistakes.

After a while, someone must have mentioned this curious fact, and they set off again, first quite possibly to Sicily, which although an island, did not measure up either, and from there to what later became known as "Spain". They may have actually gone beyond the "Pillars of Hercules" and entered the area by the River Tagus in Portugal; or conversely via the already existing Mediterranean ports. From there they gradually worked their way across the Peninsula until they reached the areas of what is now Northern Portugal, Asturias, and Galicia, either way, this green land appeared as something which even the most dense amongst them must have recognised resembled the land they had been told to expect. At this point, I must remind you that we are referring to Myth.

Generations pass. The inhabitants of the land are known as Iberians, and many place names begin to appear including the word "Iber" (which most likely means "River" but why ruin a good story at this point!) We shall refer to it again in due course.

To go back somewhat: Two new groups of people emerged in Central Europe around about the late Neolithic period. Each group may be identified independently by their respective burial sites.

The first is the so-called Beaker folk, buried with their Bell Beaker-shaped drinking vessels; the second the "Battle-Axe" folk. It is thought that they may have originated in the Middle East, perhaps as far as present-day Iran, and as separate peoples. In Central Europe, by about the beginning of the second millenium, they have fused to become one European people, though with varying cultures. Shortly afterwards, the Bronze age began.

Three successive cultures appear: the first, the Unêtice appear to be the original fusing of the Beaker and the Battle-Axe folk. The Tumulus culture followed the Unêtice, and they are distinguished, as the name implies, by their manner of burying their dead beneath burial mounds. These are to be found throughout Europe, and the British Islands are found also, scattered through Northern and Northwest Spain, and Northern and Central Portugal.

The next group to follow we know as the Urnfeld culture. Some scholars have identified these people as "Proto-Celtic" in that they may have spoken an early form of that language. These people cremated their dead and placed the remains in urns which were buried in flat cemeteries without any covering mound. Like the Tumulus people before them, this period of prehistory shows a great deal of expansion with trade to the south east and later the south west. It is during the period of the Urnfeld people that agriculture begins to thrive in south and central Europe. This was the time that the Bronze Age was at its peak. Archaeological evidence shows that they produced weapons, tools, eating and cooking vessels, etc.

By the time of the Hallstatt people (named after the town of Hallstatt in Austria where large archaeological finds have been made), and La Tene people, (named likewise after an area in western Switzerland), we find tribes who are considered fully Celtic. Their culture stretched from approximately 1200 BCE to 500 BCE, and it is the very central period which is of interest to us, for this is the period that they began to cross the western passes of the Pyrenees. Many historians argue that the Halstatt people, from whom we derive the idea of "Celtishness" may have penetrated as far as Britain, and possibly later into Ireland through Wales, but by the time they did so, those who had moved towards the Iberian Peninsula had long gone. These people that entered the Western passes through the Pyrenees appear to be an earlier group. It is thought that they did so as early as 1100 BCE. That they left a strong impression upon Iberia, especially in the north, there is no doubt.

However, there are still gaps to be explained, and it is another paper, if not a book, to attempt to explain them.

In the present Spanish provinces of Guipuzcoa,

Vizcaya, and Navarra, there is no record whatsoever of Celtic dominance, or, for that matter, any dominance at all. For these are the Basque regions. The Celts would have found themselves moving through this area, but it would appear that the local populations were sufficiently strong to resist them, or to finally absorb them and completely transform them.

As is well-known, Basque bears no resemblance to Spanish, or any other language.

Farther west, however, the Celts either displaced or dominated the older stocks of people, amongst them would have been the Iberians. Still farther west and northwest, they found people very much like themselves and they began to blend with them. The Celts wore trousers, whereas the Iberians still wore robes. It is likely that the Celts brought the domesticated horse with them and it is also just as likely that the Celtiberians adopted the Celtic mode of dress. Another point worth mentioning is that the Celts had no written language, yet the Iberians did, in some cases quite sophisticated. It is this language which has been used to identify the names of the gods inscribed throughout the northwest.

The Celts came into Iberia with their flocks, families, and wagons. Interestingly, one type of wagon is still in use in Galicia today. Like the Iberians, with whom it is more than likely they share a common racial bond originating in the Middle East, they were a pastoral people. It is difficult to determine which kind of economy was dominant - as in all countries, this is determined by the region itself, but in the northern forests there was an abundance of everything they needed for their animals - beech mast and acorns for pigs, and food for their horses, cattle, and goats. On the Meseta, the land proved perfect for the harvesting of crops, and there it was this type of farming which predominated.

The wild boar seems to have been an object of particular veneration, possibly of both groups, but certainly after the two began to meld their very similar cultures. In the northwest, several *Verracos* have been found: crude stone sculptures of life-sized pigs. These appear to date to the 6th century BCE, and are considered Celt-Iberian. However,, the veneration of the animal did not preclude its uses as a food, often perhaps as sacrificial animals, whose flesh was later enjoyed. Other animals also seemed to have been held sacred and it is noteworthy that the Irish Celts also kept sacred cattle and swine.

Although there was certainly a variation between the generally dark-haired Iberians and the taller, blonde

or red-headed Celts, both types may be seen in the
northwest today, and have quite easily identified
features which differ both from the Spanish of the
Eastern ports, and the Andalucians, which show

 considerable Moorish
influence.

Today's Galician or
Asturian, as well as
the people of Northern
Portugal, show that the
Celti-Iberians, as they became known, have
produced many descendants who occupy these
regions today. But did these earliest people call
themselves Celts?

As we have already seen, there is some conjecture
that they called themselves Iber, and that the land of
Iberia, today's Spain (which comes from Hispania,
the name given to the Peninsula by the Romans), and
subsequently Hibernia as the ancient land of Ireland,
the Land of Ir, or of Erin.

While he may not have been the first, Herodotus
mentions the Keltoi. They are also called this and

Galatai by other writers of the period and later, and it is interesting that the two names are given to essentially the same peoples. They are generally described as having fair or red hair, and blue eyes. But the same description has been attributed to the peoples of Scythia. The Romans modified this to the Celtae and the Galli. But although there were to be found throughout Europe and as far as the Black Sea, the Celts as a people do not seem to have existed. They were instead a great number of tribes who appeared to have acted, for the most part, independently of one another. There was no Celtic Emperor, nor common leader. They had no central administration, no form of government outside of what was determined individually by the tribes. They had no unified army which could be called upon in times of war against a common foe. Perhaps because the European Celts, such as they were, had no common foe. The problem of identifying who, in fact were "Celtic" and who were not and the extent of Celtic culture might be solved if we were more knowledgeable as to which of the tribes identified by the Greeks and the Romans were indigenous and which were not. This is particularly true in the Iberian Peninsula. Speaking of the Keltoi of Iberia, Herodotus identified them in a region close to the Algarve in southern Portugal, yet Aristotle claims they were above Iberia in a very cold region. Although the northwest is colder than Portugal, even during the winter, it could hardly be described as very cold - very wet, maybe. The interior of Castilla, however, can be downright chilly in the winter.

 It would appear that there is little agreement. The problem as it appears to me is that we have fallen into a tendency to think of the Celts as a clearly identifiable people, and I think I have demonstrated that this was not so. Although the term "Celtic" may mean certain common features in terms of economics, social structure, and religion, even this differs from area to

area, and likewise, since geography frequently determines character, from tribe to tribe. Only language seems to be a constant factor and it remains so today, although by this criterion - and this has kept Galicia from being accepted by the Celtic League - the so-called Celtic peoples remaining in Galicia and Asturias, are not so by contemporary definition.

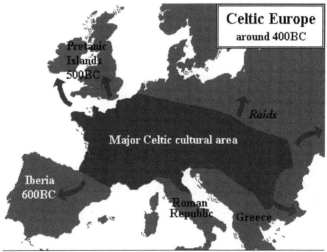

Map produced for The Ireland Story. This map may be used elsewhere provided a link is given to www.irelandstory.com, the site is non-profit and the map is not modified.

Besides, the time of Herodotus is much later than our story, so perhaps it is time to return to it.

What has been suggested, is that the inhabitants of the north-west of Spain and Portugal, began as one and the same people, originating near or east of the Black Sea. They left their homeland at some point in Biblical history, and separated near the Danube. There is good evidence which shows that these were of Indo-European stock and in fact originated in Assyria, but I shall return to this later.

It took 2000 years or more for the family reunion. By that time, Great Uncle Arthur would barely have recognised Great Aunt Maud.

And so, we are free to pick up our tale once again of how the Hibernians got to Hibernia, and what they did when they got there.

It begins with King Breoghan, a Celt-Iberian who had two sons: Ir (or Ith) and Bil. Bil had a son whose name was Mil (Milesius, from whom the Milesians are named). Breoghan had built an enormous watchtower on the north west coast of Spain.

One winter evening, Ir, Breoghan's son, stood atop the watchtower and looking northwards across the seas he saw a glistening island (Don't say I didn't warn you!). He set off with ninety warriors to investigate.

The rulers of this land were the Tuatha Dé Danann, the gods who had wrested control from the giants. They welcomed Ir and his men when he landed, but Ir was foolish enough to speak of the land in such glowing terms that the gods decided that he might have plans to take over (and yes, you have heard this story before - you would think they would have known by now). So they had Ir killed. When news of his murder reached Breoghan in Iberia, he ordered his nephew, Mil, to send his eight sons north to even up the score. They gathered an armada of sixty-five ships and sailed, arriving, legend has it, at Donegal. In their number was Scota, the wife of Mil, who was to give her name to the land of Scotland, as the Celts moved north-east. Amergin was the first to set foot upon the shore, and planting his right foot upon the soil, said: "What land is better than this island of the setting sun."

Some reports say that he cut off his right hand and threw it onto the shore from the boat so that he would be the first to touch it. One can only assume this was not his sword hand.

The Milesians agreed that this was their new home, but first they had to contend with the gods. They marched towards Tara and along the way they met with Erin, one of the goddesses and the wife of the god, MacGreine. She prophesised that the land would become theirs and asked them to name it after her and Amergin consented.

However, when they reached the home of the gods, the gods complained that they had been taken by surprise. A cry of "Not Fair" was heard upon the land. A plan was agreed upon whereby the Milesians would behave in an honourable manner and that they would once again embark on their ships, returning to a distance of nine waves from the shore. By then, the gods would be ready for battle.

But the gods played a trick on them and raised a powerful wind preventing the Milesians from reaching the shore.

This, not to put too fine a point on it, pissed Amergin off!

"I invoke the Land of Erin," he bellowed, "The shining, shining sea! The fertile hills! The wooded vales! The rivers abundant! The fishful lakes...!"

The incantation worked as the land itself rose up and forced the wind to die down.

To make an increasingly lengthy story shorter, the final result was Milesians 1 and the gods, Nil - but since Nil is an Irish name, perhaps zero might be more accurate. The gods and goddesses retreated below the earth and selected a new king, the Dagda, who allotted each member a mound beneath which the deities would engage in perpetual feasting, emerging every now and then to curdle milk, and blight corn, and so on, as crossed gods and goddesses do.

After a while of this, the new kings of Ireland decided it was in their best interests to make peace with the deities, hence they were given an honorary role - even if their palaces were below ground.

Many stories issue from here, some as tall or taller. But I shall leave those to the Irish!

And so, back to Spain.

What would life have been like for the Celt-Iberians?

One major advantage that the Celts brought with them was that they brought their plough. Although it was of little use on the highlands, it was immeasurably welcomed in the pastoral areas. Up to this point, it was women who planted seed and hoed the cereals for bread and beer (*Cerveza - Cervexa* in Gallego - is a Celtic word, by the way; Beer is Saxon). There seems to be little dissention in the association of males and ploughs and so to some degree men began to be involved in planting, which re-affirms the also universal fascination of men for tools and gadgets! Up to this point, men had considered farming unmanly and women's work. Now, they ventured out into the fields to try out their new toys and no doubt congregated in Celt-Iberian taverns to down a brew or two afterwards and discuss the relative size and efficiency of their ploughs.

And no doubt their women folk breathed a sigh of relief and went back to raising children and small animals.

In the central area around the present cities of Zamora, Valladolid and Palencia, large quantities of wheat were harvested especially by the *Vacceos*, a group living close to the Douro valley; these people came late into the peninsula and may have brought more sophisticated farming methods with them. As their name suggests, they were also raisers of cattle. These people were likely also Celts from Europe, perhaps originating in the Alsace Lorraine region. They organised into a collective society, and this made them unusual. The grain harvest was officially controlled - division was made equally and the death penalty was enacted for holding out any of the grain from the collective pool.3

In the northern mountains, there was more a combination of herding, farming, and hunting and gathering, without any particular accent upon one or the other. This remains very much the system even today in Galicia. Strabo, writing about them was surprised that they lacked olive oil (which the Etruscans and Greeks introduced to the south and east much later). In its place he said they used butter, although it was much more likely lard. The words *manteca* for pig fat and *mantequilla* for butter predate Latin and as you see are very similar in sound and derivation. In either case, there was notable dependence upon animal fat.

To this day, the north west of the Meseta, the area known as Extramadura abounds in oak trees, as does much of central Portugal and north into the area around Leon. Gathering appears to have had much importance and Strabo also mentioned that the northern people gathered great quantities of acorns, both as food for themselves and for their livestock. He neglected to mention the chestnut. There are still woods of sweet chestnut trees in this area, and the vast forests which preceded them have disappeared only in the last few generations. In the 19th century they still flourished.

Although the Iberians knew iron, and in fact the northwest abounds in this mineral, they did not seem to have known how to use it. It was the Celts who taught them how to make tools and utensils from iron. Open-cast mining would have been in evidence, and by the time the Romans came in the 2nd century BCE, the abundance of iron in the northwest would have made this a desirable area to settle and work. And they did.

Despite, Asterix the Gaul, the Celts had met their match.

*   *   *   *

In comparison to many other regions, very little is known about Celt-Iberian religious beliefs. For example, it is by no means secure that the Druids were ever in Spain, although their presence is clearly attested in Gaul, Wales, and Ireland. While many in Galicia will tell you that there were druids in their land, none of the ancient writers mention their presence in the Peninsula, although there is some conjecture that they might have been known under another name. Certainly, there were priestesses: the *Meigas*, who were the protectors of the tribe. In Ireland, the word was changed to *Machas*. All primitive societies had their shamans and it was likely that the Celt-Iberians were no exception.

Some writers have claimed that Druidism predates the Celts and that the Celts adopted it after their conquest of Britain. Either way, it would seem that Druidism in Gaul and in Ireland took on a different nature. Caesar claimed that Druidism originated in Britain independently of the Celts, and that the Gaulish Celts went there to study it.

There are, however, indications of a strict caste system between the sacred leaders or priesthood - which included the *Meigas*, the "witches", the Warriors, and the ordinary people. In fact, the distinction is so reminiscent of the Indian caste system that I cannot omit it. (The Brahmans, the Shatryas, and the Shudras, the native Dravidians becoming the untouchables.)

I shall examine the fusion of the Celtic and Iberian religions as though they were one. If similarities existed between them, then coexistence amongst them would have been facilitated, and no doubt over time, the two religions would have become one and the same, as the inscriptions would indicate.

These inscriptions abound in the areas in question, most especially around Braga in modern-day Portugal. The area just north of Braga is called Tras-O-Montes, and even today is inhospitable. The climate varies considerably and the inhabitants claim: *"Nueve meses del invierno, y tres meses del inferno"*, which translates to nine months of winter, and three months of hell! It is here that many inscriptions have been found on mountain tops and above *fuentes* - fountains, or natural springs.

These inscriptions mention gods with unpronounceable names such as: *"Aho para ligo menus"* ... as I said: unpronounceable. In some cases, there are words written in a native language - more likely Iberian than Celtic as the Celts are not known to have a written language.

The most notable deity was Endovellicus (all names given are Latin or Greek translations). There have been about fifty inscriptions found on which his name is mentioned. The centre of his cult appears to have been near Ebora in central Portugal. It is thought that he was the god of health.

The cult of Ataecina was considerably more widespread than that of Endovellicus and about 20 inscriptions have been found. One such has been discovered in Merida, which as Augusta Emerita was an important city for the Romans: largely a retirement community for soldiers. Here she has been identified with Proserpina, as both an agrarian deity and one who looked over the region of the dead. Although is thought that she was a Celtic goddess, her name is not known elsewhere where it is likely she had another, different name. On the top of a mountain near Braga, an inscription has been found to Distercio, whilst other inscriptions have been found in the mountains of the same region, including one to the god, Brigus, an Iberian name. It is thought that this Brigus may later have been identified with Jupiter, and may have been the same as the Celtic god Lug, after whom Lugudunum in Gaul (present day Lyons in France) was named and also at Lugo in Galicia.

Jupiter was especially revered in Lugo which was a garrison town. Lug was a deity who presided over a neighboring mountain.

As an aside, although there are almost no traces of Romans worshipping the local gods, some Roman soldiers seem to have written their names on inscriptions to Vagdonaegus, who was likely a Celt-Iberian god, though of what, we do not know. Again, these were found near Lugo at Astorga in the Province of Leon.

There are clear traces of worship of river gods, most

especially in the north and west. An inscription to the god Durius, who rules the river Douro, has been found. Also, five inscriptions to the goddess Nabia have been discovered, and her name lives on in the river Navia which crosses Asturias and arises on the border with Galicia. Many inscriptions have been found over mountain springs. On several there is a picture of what is likely the river god. In one case, one of the previously mentioned unpronounceable gods (Tongo-ena-biacus) appears holding in his left hand a basket of fruit. Water sprites were also thought to have watched over fountains and I shall return to them later. Wheat stalks and bread were often given at these fountains as an offering.

Among the many inscriptions to Endovellicus are several which indicate that the natives revered rocks and stones. Even in the worship of the river gods and goddesses, it may have been the central stone above the spring which was the object of worship. From here, no doubt, we have retained our practice of throwing pennies - as offering stones to propitiate the denizen within. On the promontory of Cabo San

Vicente, at the extreme SW of Portugal, there is to this day a superstition against remaining there at night because it was thought that the gods occupied it at that time. The souls of the dead were thought to inhabit certain stones which, if turned about, could cause rain.

Stones, and especially cairns along roadsides and at intersections are still to be found in abundance in northern Spain. On one particularly difficult stretch of the Camino de Santiago, thousands of these have been laid one upon the other at intervals and the result is nothing less than a stone garden. These were the gods to be honoured when travel was to be undertaken. Again, on the Camino, not far from Lugo is an iron pole, topped with a cross. Beneath it lies a pile of stones more than 20 feet high left there by pilgrims which probably predate the so-called discovery of Saint James tomb in Compostela by hundreds of years. The site was designated as a place for the worship of Mercury by the Romans, but as Mercury was little venerated in Spain (far more in France) one wonders who was the original god whose Celtic or Iberian name is now lost to us. This area, by the way, abounds in iron, and the site is called the Cruz de Ferro. (or "Hierro") being a local word for iron.

About one hundred and thirty Celtic and Iberian gods and goddesses are, however, known to us by name, and of those 230 inscriptions have been found. Some bear the suffix "- *briga", "-brigus",* or *aecus, or aegus* and these are thought to be older, Iberian gods. Others such as Matres, Lugoves, and Epona, the goddess of horses are undoubtedly Celtic and have been found near La Coruña, most likely the area where the Milesians and their descendants settled. This would appear to indicate that by the time of the northerly migration (if indeed there was one), the Celts, with their horses, had arrived.

If you go to visit the provinces of Asturias or Galicia today, you will likely encounter the *Xanas*. These were the Old Ones, the Fairy Folk, and even today, they are treated with a great deal of respect, for one cannot be too careful, after all. The *Xanas* (or Danas, or Dianas, as they have also been called) occupy the fountains and streams, and sometimes the forests and trees; less frequently in caves. They are related to Indo-European myths of a similar kind, and the Sylvan goddess of the Romans. Some are thought to have children of their own, the *Xaniños,* and not wishing to raise them themselves, left them with nursing mothers. To avoid this, mothers would leave eggshells in pots, or the skin of an apple in their baby's beds.

Another ancient elf is the Culiebre, also a dragon spirit from the Indo-European regions. He was said to live in caves or under waterfalls where he guarded unknown treasures. The only moment to surprise the Culiebre was to wait until St. John's Day (the summer solstice) when the dragon would fall asleep. This was the time to remove the treasure.

I think I would have passed on this one. There are many legends surrounding it. In one, a Culiebre was terrifying the inhabitants of the Asturian region of Brañaseca (now called Cudillero on the north coast and highly reminiscent of a Cornish fishing village). The Culiebre had only one vulnerably spot and that was its throat. One day a brave young man threw bread stuffed with a red-hot stone. The greedy dragon swallowed it and died immediately. And this, of course, is just one more instance of dragon stories and the Celtish people.

The Trasno, also known in Cantabria as the Trasgu, was a character known throughout Europe and also suspected as having originated in the Indo-European stories. He is often depicted as a cripple with a horny tail, short in stature, and wearing a bright red cap. He has a  hole in his hand. He can move into your house and cause a great deal of disturbance: breaking pots, frightening livestock, and generally being very noisy at night. Moving house won't solve the problem. The Trasgu moves in with you and sings: "To your new house

you have fled, but I will follow with my cap red."
No doubt it was better in Scythian, or whatever.

Anyway, just in case you ever do encounter a Trasgu, you will need to carry a wicker basket full of water, or linseed oil; if that doesn't work, you will need to whiten a black goatskin and that ought to do the trick!

One inescapable feature of rural life in Asturias and Galicia is the raised *Horreos*: grain storage barns perched upon legs above head height - sometimes there are 6 legs, sometimes 8 and this distinction changes the name. One characteristic year-round in these north western provinces is humidity. For generations, mice and moths have been a common enemy. Yet they are venerated with festivals which first appeared in the literature of the Romans who observed celebrations of Paganalia. The horreos raise the corn and vegetables up above the ground and thus, at least in principle, they are preserved throughout the winter months. Honouring the mice

and the moths was an additional safeguard. So was the practice of putting food for the demons at the beginning of the year, the assumption being that the bad spirits would eat what had been given them and leave the rest alone. Such food was often left in hollow tree trunks.

As we have already seen, by the time the Romans arrived, the Celts and the Iberians had become indistinguishable. Dominant genes had rendered a good proportion of the population as they are: handsome, quite finely boned people, quite dark-haired for the most part, but many blue or green-eyed people are found, and most have fair skin. Red and blonde-haired types are still to be found, whereas they are rare in the southern and eastern provinces, at least they were until the tourists arrived!

It would appear that the Romans had far less to do with these northern people than they did with other races. For the most part, life went on as normal, and the old gods were still revered. Sometimes Roman customs such as having a household god were followed, especially in more wealthy families. Sometimes, as we have seen, Native and Roman gods were conflated; sometimes re-named, sometimes hyphenated.

Of interest, there have been twelve inscriptions to Isis and Serapis, especially in northern Portugal and Galicia. In some cases, these have been joined with Jupiter.

By the time Christianity came to Spain, there were few changes to be seen in the northern and western regions. Many were nominally Christians, but in an area which is predominantly rural, changes come slowly, and the Roman church had little impact.

There were, however, dioceses throughout Spain, mostly concentrated in the south and east, but Lusitania (modern-day Portugal), Galicia (Finis Terrae - the Land's End by the Romans), and Asturias was no exceptions. In the 4th century, the Emperor Constantine, after having seen a cross in the sky at the Battle of Milvian - and supposedly hearing a voice promising him victory - had afterwards decreed that there would be one God. One God, that is, and One Emperor. Needless to say, such a conversion was expedient and anyway shortly afterwards he murdered members of his family. It is said that on his deathbed he converted to Christianity.

The Council of Elviria, near modern day Granada, met in 315 CE to discuss what to do about Christians, especially Christians who had claim to the priesthood, who couldn't seem to make their minds up as to whether they were Christians or Pagans. Although the Council considered the vestiges of Roman paganism to be of greater concern (since the south was thoroughly Romanised by that time), Bishops from the north and west attended, including a bishop from Galicia. Several pagan practices were discussed. Certain pagan customs such as keeping vigil by the dead, bringing a feast to help the spirit to pass on, or at anniversary dates. (This latter is still celebrated in November, All Souls Day, where the families take a picnic to the cemetery. It is a National Holiday.) Women lighting candles and spending the night hours at gravesites were of special concern, as were other non-Christian practices notably Celtic in nature. One which subsequently got up the noses of bishops at a later council was the practice by some inhabitants of rural areas farther to the north, of wearing goat skins, and sometimes deerskins with antlers.

Many high members of the priesthood indulged in practices less than spiritual, (though dressing in skins does not appear to be one of them) and these included one Bishop of Augusta Emerita (Merida) who by 379 had been indicted by many of his peers for having produced children in secret, and much general high-handed behaviour. Which, as our story unfolds, included physically harming two bishops from neighbouring dioceses who came to have a friendly chat. This was the genesis of the so-called Priscillian heresy which came very close to ousting the Roman church from the north and west and continued in Galicia in particular for at least 200 years after Priscillian's death.

Priscillian, a noble Roman of considerable wealth who had likely been at one time a Senator, gathered an enormous following in the north and west. His preaching, which it would seem particularly appealed to those who still followed the Old Gods, or who had only nominal affinity for mainstream Christianity, was certainly unorthodox, and included such practices as retreating into the hills in groups and alone, and spiritual community in conventicles. He may, in fact, have used Celtic pagan practices in his ministry, (one of the charges against him was that he conducted services in the fields and barefoot) and was undoubtedly influenced by the Gnosticism of the Eastern Mediterranean. Many of his followers were women, who were treated equally with men. No clergy were elected; instead, votes were taken from meeting to meeting to decide who would preside.

Yet, corruption continued in orthodox circles and when the See of Avila became vacant, Priscillian was persuaded, though a layman, to accept it. By this time he had made many enemies, as you may imagine, and he was brought up on charges. Although he claimed that his ministry contained nothing that was not contained in the Holy Books, he had studied much apocryphal material and was likely entirely familiar with those lost writings (which incidentally disappeared in Egypt at about the time of Priscillian's death) which we have come to call the Gnostic Gospels: The Nag Hammadi Codices. He and two of his following took their case to the emperor, at that time, Gratian, and for a while, the charges against him were dropped. He returned to Spain and continued to attract huge numbers of followers, especially in his native Galicia. It was only a matter of time.

With the death of Gratian at the hands of Maximus, Hydatius of Merida, along with Ithacius of Ossunuba, complained once again to the new emperor. Maximus needed money. He had exhausted his treasury in battles against Gratian, and the Priscillianists, not excluding Priscillian himself, were a ready source of cash. Priscillian and six of his followers, including Euchrotia a wealthy widow from Gaul, were ordered to Treveris, modern day Trier, near Luxembourg.

He and his followers were charged with Manicheeism, by a civil court. Although this would have been considered a severe heresy, it was not a capital crime. However, added to this was the use of pagan rites within a Christian ministry, the practice of Astrology, the procuring of abortions, witchcraft and magic, the last of which carried the death penalty.

All seven were decapitated in 385 CE. It is the first instance whereby a Christian was put to death by

Christians. After three years, and after the downfall of Maximus, Priscillian's followers were allowed permission to bring the body back to Spain. There is evidence that it might have been brought to Galicia and that it was Priscillian's body, along with two of his followers, which was discovered in the place called Compostela in the early 9th century. But that is another story...

It took over two hundred years, until the area was over-run by the Visigoths, before there is no longer any mention of Priscillianism, despite the best efforts of the Roman Catholic Church.

*   *   *   *

Finally, and briefly, to return to the Hebrews...

There are many place names in France and Britain which begin with Eber, Aber, or Iber. While it is true that this word does appear to indicate a river, there is still a lingering amount of potential evidence pointing to a Middle-Eastern, Indo-European origin for our Celts, Gaels, and Iberians and Hibernians. In addition to Yair Davidiy, who until recently has appeared as a lone voice in the wilderness, Assyrian tablets dating from the 8th century BCE have recently been assembled which might indicate the direction the dispersion of the Lost Tribes may have taken. The tablets written in cuneiform appear to tell the story of how the Hebrews were initially welcomed in another land- although Egypt is not named - later kept captive, and then having escaped, dispersed throughout Europe and the Mediterranean basin. It has been suggested that some of these people were the Asshur of Assyria, named after the son of the Biblical Shem. These people were known to occupy a city in Mesopotamia on the lower Tigris which they called "Kir". They were also known as the Kahtti, (which I have been told is a German word for Hebrew...?).

*   *   *   *

Celticism today is big business, and Galicia and Asturias are no exceptions to the rest of those areas considered "Celtic". If you go to the north of Spain, you will hear music played on the *Gaïta* - the

Gallego bagpipes - which is virtually indistinguishable from Irish music although there is a certain North African influence which marks it out, as do some of the more unusual instruments. A version of the borghan was, and still is played not only in most parts of North Africa, but also as far east as Iran, and possibly in isolated pockets still further; the tin whistle is readily heard in the horns of Morocco. You will see original artwork of traditional "Celtic" design - but I must tell you that you will see it also in Egypt, and Syria, and the maze in Iran, Afghanistan, and India. You will drink cider in Asturias, you will see mountains and rivers which will remind you of Wales, and coastlines reminiscent of Cornwall.

You will see dolmens and burial mounds and hear the story of the little people, who live below the ground. But the one thing you won't see - at least not outside of the inevitable tourist shops, is the Celtic cross.

That one, it seems, belongs to St. Patrick alone.

Footnotes:

1: Although they are somewhat outside of the scope of this paper, I think worth a mention the "Guanches" peoples of the Canary Islands, who were thought to have migrated from North Africa at some time in pre-history, and were still there at the time the first Celts from the European regions began to arrive through the Pyrenean passes. They left hundreds of cave sites: 300 in one mountain alone. There is also a suggestion that they may have been the remnants of the Atlantean civilization, but not with a very large barge pole would I touch upon that subject.

2: There are three interesting and well-preserved exceptions situated close together at Antequera, near Málaga in Andalucia, and also examples of very early cave art at the Cueva de la Pileta and others nearby. They blended with the population, which was most notably almost entirely a now firmly-rooted and agricultural group of communities.

3: Of interest is that this region and that just to the north and northwest still has a collectivist system of farming, both for wheat and for grapes. The area along the Douro valley is famous for its wine, especially white wine.

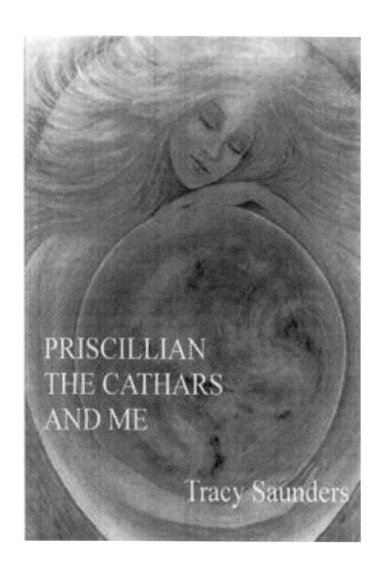

PRISCILLIAN
THE CATHARS
AND ME

Tracy Saunders

Imagery ©2015 Data SIO, NOAA, U.S. Navy, NGA, GEBCO, Landsat, IBCAO, U.S. Geological Survey, Map data   100 km
©2015 GeoBasis-DE/BKG (©2009), Google, Inst. Geogr. Nacional

Direct route from Galicia to the south of Ireland

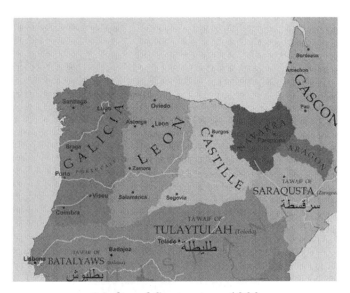

Medieval Spain circa 1200

Priscillian, the Cathars and Me

Tracy Saunders

Prologue

When I was approached by Brock University to give a paper at a conference on Gnosticism, I asked: What sort of thing would you like me to speak about? Just say why you like Gnosticism, was the reply.

I have to admit that I found this really amusing. I mean I can tell you why I like sushi, old Volvos, the colour green, high-heeled snakeskin boots and watching re-runs of Top Gear, and strolling in the rain, but "like" Gnosticism?

So. taking my brief literally I am going to try to explain here why Gnosticism makes sense to me personally, so much so that I think I can say that I "like" it better than mainstream Christianity, and why I could not describe myself as a Christian. Certainly, and I hope you will begin to see why, it makes far more sense. It satisfies the intellect, offers practical advice on how to live, and has its own beautiful mythology which appeals to a longing for glimpses of the ineffable which go way back to my early childhood.

A Child's Garden of Gnosticism

When I was four, I dreamt I met Jesus outside of our local village pub. He was nice, but neither meek, nor mild; quite stern in fact. I remember waking up with a sense that Jesus was telling me somehow to be very wary of what I was going to be taught.

As I grew, I devoured the Narnia chronicles of CS Lewis, which were just then being published, never once considering that Lewis was providing my thirsty young mind with allegory. It didn't matter. To this day I maintain that I learned about honour, valour, love and nobility from the children in the books and their mentor, Aslan. He made more sense to me than Jesus.

Skip forward to age 12 and my first year of secondary school. In divinity class we had to write a composition about Jesus' visit to Jerusalem as a young boy. I decided to use a bit of licence and described the excitement of the young boys at the vanguard of the group of parents who followed behind. Just imagine, I thought, how they might have behaved each one vying to be the first to see the "spires" of the city. "I saw it first," says one; "No, I did," says Jesus. I was really proud if it when I handed it in and waited for the high grade I knew must come.

Now I've always written well; it comes naturally to me and so I was excited when the teacher handed back all of the compositions with the exception of mine. I can remember to this day the exact seat I was in, waiting with great anticipation to hear what a remarkable insight I had had into the everyday life of Jesus.

I was to be not only disappointed but roundly embarrassed in front of twenty-five other girls all of which had their papers on the desk in front of them.

"But," said the teacher, "there is one that I simply must read out to you all," and picking up my composition began to tell my story. I was thrilled. At last, acknowledgement for my hard work and imagination.

Then she finished. And turned on me in such a fashion as I had never seen. How **dare** I treat the Lord Jesus as though he were a normal child, what **blasphemy** was this in her own class...she went on and on.

One part of me just wanted to slide under the desk and stay there for the next five years. But you know, the other part of me wanted to scream: "**You are so wrong!**"

Rather than give up, I began to read the bible independently. One of the first things I encountered was the bit in Genesis where Adam and Eve slink off to the Land of Nod, procreate, struggle with their unfortunate lot, and eventually watch their children find their own wives.

Huh?

Where did they come from? Even a teenage brain can do process of elimination:

a/ God created some more people? Doesn't say that anywhere

b/ Cain and Abel married their sisters? Ditto. Scandalous and forbidden too.

c/ Cain and Abel went off somewhere and came back with their brides. Red light, red light...does not compute.

I began to read of a vengeful, vindictive and by his own admission "jealous" God (of whom?) who appeared to set up poor Adam and Eve - and especially Eve - right from the beginning just to make sure that they were stupid enough not to use the intellect he had somehow given them, and then had a temper tantrum when they did. I read of other gods... Wait a minute, haven't they been ramming down my throat that there is only one? Most of all I read that God was everywhere, all powerful, all knowing...all good.

Not the one I had been reading about.

I dropped God like a hot potato. And Jesus the revolutionary too.

Many, many years later, while working in a bookshop, I unpacked a box of books that had come in that morning. Out came a slim volume called The Gnostic Gospels. I sat back on the carpet and opened it up. I began to get the idea: Jesus actually said far more than what we had read in the New Testament. Many new "gospels" had been discovered years before and now they had only recently been translated into English. They included, Peter, Thomas, Mary even. I took the book home that night and read it from cover to cover.

Now I would like to say that my life changed from that moment, but it didn't. Pagel's book, however, did alert me to the fact that there was more to

Christianity than I had so far been taught, that what was contained in these books helped to explain more about what I had rejected. In fact, Jesus DID seem to have a message that fitted in with my spiritual cravings. Like Mary Magdalene, I wanted to be the woman who knew the all.

This took me to philosophy where I learned to ask the right questions. But it wasn't enough.

I slipped back to my agnostic state. It would be a while before I met someone who challenged me to truly move forward on my spiritual quest.

With the publication of my first novel, Pilgrimage to Heresy, and before, I have been asked many times why I decided to walk the Camino de Santiago and to this day I can't give a definitive answer. I like the one given by Jack Hitt in his wonderful book Off the Road". When, as he is about to get his Compostela at the cathedral he is asked his reasons for walking the the Camino de Santiago he replies: "To find out my reasons for walking." I would have to say those were mine too.

Along the Way of St. James, I met a man from Salt Lake City, Utah. We walked and talked about the nature of pilgrimage in a secular age. "You know, Tracy,": he said, "the chances are that it is not St. James buried in the cathedral anyway."

I was a bit miffed. "What do you mean?" I said, stopping. "If old Santiago isn't there, why am I walking 760 kilometres to see him?"

Lance Owens, who I was later to find out was a priest of the Gnostic church as well as an M.D. and teacher of Jung at the University of Utah, mentioned this name beginning with a "Pru-" something adding that he had been written about in a scholarly book by an Oxford professor, and I can remember very clearly a sensation that said: "That's it! That's what you have been waiting for." Unfortunately, I forgot the name immediately and it wasn't until a year later that I decided to begin my investigation. I wrote to Dr. Owens.

Priscillian, he wrote back: Priscillian Bishop of Avila.

* * * * *

Who was Priscillian of Avila?

Very little is known about Priscillian's life. Most of what we have comes from various Catholic sources, and not surprisingly, they are not sympathetic. Sulpicius Severus wrote about Priscillian, and also wrote the earliest biography of St. Martin of Tours. Martin, while a follower of the traditional Roman church of the time, was severely critical of the judgement meted out to Priscillian and his followers, and petitioned Maximus the Emperor to call off the inquisition sent to Spain after Priscillian's execution. This, not surprisingly, led to accusations that Martin was secretly a Priscillianist sympathiser himself.

By far the best contemporary source of information about Priscillian's thought and writing, and what little historical detail we do have, comes from Priscillian of Avila: The Occult and the Charismatic in the Early Church (OUP 1976) by Prof. Henry Chadwick, Regius Professor of Divinity at both Oxford and Cambridge. It is this book that Lance Owens had mentioned to me. In the last ten years, information about Priscillian has increased tenfold on the Internet although unfortunately much of it is still taken from Catholic sources such as the 1906 Catholic Encyclopaedia which is hardly sympathetic.

Pilgrimage to Heresy does not claim to give an accurate account of Priscillian's life; it is a work of fiction written to entertain, and hopefully encourage questions. However, Priscillian's religious views, by and large, are taken from the Wurzburg Tractates discovered by Georg Schepps in 1885 and published at the Vienna Corpus in 1886, and which are covered in some depth in Prof. Chadwick's book. More recently, Mario Conti's translation into English was published February 2010 as The Complete Works of Priscillian of Avila (OUP) and is gaining a good deal of notice as this is the first-time scholars have had the chance to read Priscillian's words in anything other than Latin or German. Since he was, and to some extent still is, especially venerated in Galicia, and since it seems highly likely that he was brought there for burial - which of course is the main thesis of my novel - I believe that there are some grounds for claiming this part of northern Spain as his birthplace and I am by no means alone in this. That he was executed in Trier in either 385 or 386 CE is beyond doubt, although it is worth mentioning here that at a visit to the cathedral in Avila while I was researching the book, I approached a priest there and enquiring about information about Priscillian I was told that "no such person ever existed"! Now there are only two explanations for this. Either this priest was ignorant of the history of his own church, which I very much doubt, or, he was lying through his Catholic teeth. The decapitation of Priscillian and some of his followers in Trier was the first case of capital punishment through the Catholic "inquisition" in the history of the Church.

Priscillian was clearly influenced by some sort of doctrine, or perhaps, as I have suggested, a book of some kind. He was visited by a woman who called herself Agape, and a man named Elpidius, who had come from Egypt. These two purportedly had become friendly with a man named Marcus of Memphis, who had connections with Gnosticism. When I first read Professor Chadwick's book, I knew that this story was too good to remain in theological and scholastic obscurity. It was the stuff of best-sellers and I knew I would have to write it myself. The result was Pilgrimage to Heresy which has now been translated into Spanish and published as *Peregrinos de la Herejia*. Priscillian gathered an immense following. His message brought men and women from all walks of life to his gnostic message of salvation, and not only from Galicia but throughout Spain, especially the north, into the south of France and even the northern states of Italy. For the Priscillianists, friendship with the world was friendship with the devil and thus enmity with God. He who called himself the Creator God was deluding himself since he had originated in a lie; however, humankind could not blame the Devil for his sins as he did retain free-will and had an obligation to extricate his soul from its earthly bondage by the practice of true Christianity and the reading and study of the Bible, `day and night`. Merely nominal Christianity was not enough. The resurrection of the body, Priscillian taught, was achieved by the realisation of the spirit. Thus, by implication, th there could be no bodily resur-rection of Christ in the literal sense. The material world, he wrote is `short-lived and evil`. Finally, and perhaps most importantly, the true God would eventually reclaim all spirits back to his bosom and this earthly realm, and the false, blind trickster Samael would cease to be. The Priscillianists were vegetarians, abstained from wine, and practiced voluntary poverty and celibacy. Priscillian said that men and women were equal as their spirits were equal and that slavery was horrific and must be abolished. We are talking 1700 years ago here!

Not surprisingly, he had enemies. Priscillian's most notable opponents were Hydatius of Emerita Augusta (present day Merida), and Ithacius of Ossonuba (present day Faro in the south of Portugal). Between them, they petitioned Gratian, the then Emperor (soon to be killed by Maximus "The Usurper", who denied any involvement in Gratian's death), and a Synod was held at Saragossa (Zaragoza in Spain) in 381. The Synod was not well attended, however, which begs the question as to whether Hydatius and Ithacius' charges were of much interest to the rest of the Iberian bishops, and neither Priscillian, nor any of his followers attended. A late message from the Pope absolved the Priscillianists of all possible charges since they had not been there to defend themselves. They were most certainly not, as I have read on the Internet, "ex-communicated" at this Synod, as was put about by Priscillian's accusers.

It was well known that Hydatius had a wife and likely one or more children. He kept himself surrounded with a mafia-like protection unit. Many of his congregation had refused to take communion with him. But he was clearly disturbed at the Priscillianist presence and wrote to his Metropolitan Ithacius to complain. After a Priscillianist delegation by Bishops Instantius and Salvianus to Hydatius in Merida was turned away - and in which, the bishops were bodily thrown out of Hydatius' presence - they appointed Priscillian Bishop of Ávila. Appalled and likely worried for their own survival, Hydatius and Ithacius appealed to the Emperor Gratian, who issued a rescript threatening the Priscillianists with banishment. Consequently, the three Priscillian bishops went in person to Rome, to present their case before Damasus the Pope. Despite being refused an audience with either pope or emperor, some exchange of what was likely a considerable amount of money to the imperial *questor* secured the restoration of their churches.

Ithacius, Priscillian's main accuser, fled to Trier fearing that he would answer himself for his charges against a fellow bishop. But the die was cast. What had essentially begun as a church matter, now attracted the attention of the secular arm. It was ultimately to prove Priscillian's downfall. The murder of Emperor Gratian in Lyon and the accession, at Trier (Trèves, in Germany) of the usurper Magnus Maximus (383) was to cause the tide to turn against the Priscillianists. Maximus was a soldier who had no interest in church matters, but he was bound to listen to Ithacius' - who was now returned from exile - complaints. In consequence of his representations a new synod was held (384) at Bordeaux. The Priscillianists had dangerous enemies in the Aquitaine and faced a hung jury. Instantius was sent into exile in the Scilly Isles. Salvianus had died while the Priscillianists were in Rome and so was spared the questioning. Priscillian, knowing that his protestations would meet with no sympathetic hearers, appealed directly to Maximus, but the emperor had other concerns to deal with, not least of which building up his coffers after an expensive war. Going directly to meet with then new emperor was clearly a grave mistake as the charges against Priscillian now included witchcraft as well as heresy, and witchcraft was a capital crime. The Priscillianists had estates, money; Maximus needed to pay his war debts. He had no need of further difficulties with his bishops and even less interest in church matters. Instead of receiving the fair hearing they expected, their case was handed over to the secular arm for judgement. Priscillian's execution could only benefit the emperor who was seriously short of cash. He made no move to stop the court proceedings. Priscillian and his followers, including Eucrotia, the widow of a Roman noble with estates at Elusa in southern France, was beheaded at Trier in either 385 or 386, the first Christians martyred by those who were Christians themselves. Ambrose of Milan, Pope Siricius, and Martin of Tours protested against Priscillian's execution. But Priscillian had, fatally, presented his case outside of the ecclesiastical court for "justice"; his persecutors had made a case for witchcraft and sorcery as well as heresy; and the former was a capital crime. For us today, the charges themselves may seem innocent enough: Priscillian had more than likely participated in some age-old ritual common in the countryside which had clung to the old ways. Perhaps he was observed by someone for whom this was interpreted as a direct threat to the newly formed Roman Church. Perhaps that person or persons had an agenda of their own. We simply cannot determine truth from falsehood at this point. Priscillian's "confession" was extracted under torture. He confessed to "magical" practices, meetings at night with women, and praying naked. All of these were likely true. But it was the demonic interpretation put upon them by the Catholic

 inquisitors which were to lead to the death penalty. Priscillian and six of his closest followers, including Euchrotia were executed according to the Roman law. However, Priscillianism, despite the very strict measures taken by Maximus to contain it, continued to spread in Gaul, especially on both sides of the foothills of the Pyrenees, as well as in Spain in general, and northern Spain in particular. For at

least another hundred and fifty years we hear of synod after synod convened with the express purpose of dealing with the still existent Priscillianists. In 405, The Synod of Carthage, for example, endorsed use of force by the state if persuasion failed to convert the heretics. These were not exclusively Priscillianist as there were many deviations from the state religion of Roman Catholicism by this. Some simply vanished; some were absorbed into mainstream Catholicism. However, Priscillian was long honored as a martyr, not as a heretic, especially in Galicia and what is now northern Portugal, where his body was reverentially returned from Trier. Prof. Chadwick and others, including myself, have made the tentative claim that the remains found in the early 9th century at the site rededicated to Saint James the Great— Santiago de Compostela—belong not to the apostle at all but to Priscillian. This, of course, is the mainstay of the historical thread of Pilgrimage to Heresy. With the Sueve occupation of Galicia, Priscillianism was more or less tolerated especially since the rejection of the Trinity was shared by both the Sueves who practiced Arianism and the Priscillianists, although initially, in the opening years of the fifth century, the barbarian invasions of Spain threw the whole Peninsula into confusion as the Sueves were for the most part pagan upon their entry into Spain. But those that followed mainstream Christianity were permitted to worship according to their own practices.

When they founded their kingdom in Galicia in 464, Arianism was the State religion rather than Roman Catholicism. There is nothing to suggest that the Arian bishops at this time were active in suppressing paganism. Priscillianism was tolerated as many of its beliefs were similar in fact to the state religion, and it was not until St. Martin of Braga (not to be confused with St. Martin of Tours), the Apostle of the Sueves, that Priscillianism is seen to be driven back underground. It is only after Recared the Visigoth's conversion to Catholicism in the mid-7th century that we cease altogether to hear anything about the Priscillianists. But where did they go? Did they simply die out, or be absorbed by the Catholic Church, a church notably antipathetic and entirely different to their views? Or did the movement go underground, only to re-appear as a synthesis somewhere else, somewhere were Priscillianism had had a distinct foothold 800 years before? Did Priscillian survive in the guise of the Good Men?

The Hunting of Heretics

The term "Cathars" was never used by those who simply called themselves *Les Bonhommes,* or Good Christians. While some scholars have claimed the word comes from the Greek Kataroi, meaning the Pure Ones, others, most notably Nicolas Gouzy of the *Centre d'Etudes Cathares* in France, have suggested that the name was more comparable to an insult deriving from the German *"die Ketzerei"* meaning "cat worshippers" and indeed in the iconography of the Middle Ages they were almost always accompanied by cats, a symbol of evil for all of Christendom at the time. They have also been often referred to as The Albigenses, after the chronicler Geoffrey of Vigeous in 1181, especially in the scholarly literature. But this too may be a misnomer as the town of Albi was not notably Cathar with the greatest concentration of believers to the south and south east of the Languedoc and towards the foothills of the eastern Pyrenees.

Why were the Cathars (and for ease of recognition, I'll use this term throughout) such a threat to the Roman church that it was deemed necessary to persecute and exterminate them in their hundreds, perhaps thousands?

Notable in the Cathar writings of the 13th century we find this:

> The Roman church is not ashamed to say that they are the lambs of Christ. They say that the heretics they persecute are the church of wolves. But this is absurd. The wolves have always pursued and slaughtered the sheep. It would have to be the contrary for the sheep to be so mad as to hunt down and kill the

wolves, and for the wolves to be so passive and patient as to let the sheep devour them.

The early 11th century brought about a crisis of faith. The world had not ended with the Millennium as most expected it to do according to prophecy. The clergy were seen as corrupt, seeking only power and riches; the Latin litany droned on with no-one understanding a word. No-one spoke Latin anymore and comprehension of the mass was reserved only for those who could read and write in that language; this did not even seem to include some of the priests themselves who used only well-used psalms and prayer books. In fact, as I shall mention later, the ownership of a bible was a capital offence since it pre-supposed heretical interests! People began to speak openly of the inconsistencies of the Catholic faith and Catholic practices. They spoke out about the usury of the church; of the fees collected by avaricious churchmen and their superstitious rites. The moneys they collected for holy water, oil, and earth for burial. Ordinary people began to move away from the massive cathedrals and abbeys and began to go - as the comedian Lenny Bruce has termed the 20th century spiritual comparison, "back to God".

What can the world be other than created by the devil, they said. They began to preach detachment from this realm whose prince was Satan and sought ways to "a new heaven, and a new earth where justice will dwell". In this culturally and spiritually explosive atmosphere there appeared, seemingly in the early years of the 1100's an extraordinary movement whose Christian beliefs were noticeably different from those of the Catholics. It spread like a wildfire and lasted, with its believers living quite comfortably side by side with Catholics, for many years, but as they began to attract the notice of the papal church it became the custom to refer to them as "Manichaeans", just as the charges against Priscillian had also been that he was a follower of the Persian prophet Mani.

Despite what we have read about the throwing of early Christian martyrs to the lions, this was confined to relatively short periods of time and very specific emperors. A far worse fate was exclusion within the church. Early church writers seem to agree that religious liberty up to a certain point was a matter of personal choice. Hence, we find Tertullian in the 3rd century in *Ad Scapulum* writing:

It is a fundamental human right, a privilege of nature, that every man should worship according to his own convictions. One man's religion neither harms nor helps another man. It is assuredly no part of religion to compel religion - to which free will and not force should lead us.

Soon after the adoption of Christianity as the state religion of Rome the persecution of people for holding different religious opinions began. In the year 380, Theodosius, soon after his baptism into Roman Catholicism, issued, with is co-emperors, following edict which is worth quoting in full:

We, the three emperors, will that our subjects steadfastly adhere to the religion which was taught by St. Peter to the Romans...let us believe in one Godhead of the Father, the Son, and the Holy Ghost, of equal majesty in the Holy Trinity. We order that the adherents of this faith be called Catholic Christians. We brand all the senseless followers of the other religio0ns with the infamous name of heretics,and forbid their conventicles assuming the name of churches. Besides the condemnation of divine justice, they must expect the heaviest penalties which our authority, guided by heavenly wisdom, shall think proper to inflict.

For the most part this meant excommunication. This was a serious matter. Ex-communication meant exclusion from God and delivery to Satan. It meant everlasting death, a far worse thing to countenance than simply the taking of life. However, in 381, Christians requested the emperor to strip the Manichaeans of their civil rights. By the end of the following year, the death penalty had been pronounced for all the Manichees. They were accused of magical and obscene practices. And within five years of Theodosius' edict, the "heaviest penalty" had been enacted on Priscillian, Euchrotia and the others.

By applying this name of heretic, it was a simple step to branding the Cathars as a dualist movement, inspired from the east, and thus led to them being also referred to as "false prophets": heretics for whom the ultimate penalty of burning was appropriate, if they did not immediately recant, "to save their souls". After Constantine the emperor in Rome had "converted" to Christianity, the church achieved the highest power over life and death: those who lapsed from the state religion could be saved from eternal perdition by torturing and if necessary putting them death as cruelly as possible! A law of 407 against the Donatists puts heretics on the same level as traitors to the emperor. The punishment for treason was to be burnt alive. Such extraordinary thinking allowed the Roman church to accuse, and arrange for the torture and murder of those who sought to exercise their "choice" - the true meaning of the Greek word "*hairesis*", and with a clear and divinely- justified conscience that they were acting in the best interests of the accused! In this way, of course, the Dominican friars in the 13th and later centuries were able to carry out their gruesome and loathsome task with impunity, afterwards handing over the sacrificial victim to the secular authorities for burning.

And so to return to the time of the Cathar persecutions, perhaps what worried the church most of all was the translation of the Bible into the vernacular. In France, this meant *Provencal* and the *Langue d'Oc* (quite literally the Language of Yes). Magee, in Heresy and the Inquisition, says that by 1100 educated people were starting to read the bible by themselves, but the Pope was roundly against it. If people could read God's words for themselves, they might begin to doubt or to dispute the Catholic practices which were not in line with the scriptures. Magee claims that the Popes wanted to see the power of the church, , which was their own power, dominating mens' lives. He quotes the novelist HG Wells in saying:

"It was just because many of them secretly doubted the soundness of their vast and elaborate doctrinal

fabric that they would brook no discussion of it. They were intolerant of doubts and questions, not because they were sure of their faith, but because they were unsure."

The church forbade the reading of the bible. Catholic Christians were forbidden from reading the bible, or possessing one in any language, including Latin! Theological discussion with Jews was expressly forbidden since there was no such prohibition in the Jewish faith. St. Louis admonished any Christian upon hearing of the law from a Jew to "thrust his sword into the Jew's belly as far as it will go". It was tantamount to proof of heresy that anyone would feel the need to look for proof of the church's teachings by resorting to bible study. In England, William Tyndale was burned as a heretic for translating the Bible into English and anyone owning or reading his translation was treated likewise. Not surprisingly, the various translations into the vernacular in the Aquitaine and the southern regions of France had to be stopped and *touted de suite!*

So who were the Cathars and what did they believe?

The Cathar Heresy
The Cathars or Albigenses lived, worked and preached in the areas of France from Toulouse to Beziers and from Albi to Foix in the foothills of the Pyrenees. There were, of course, Cathars outside of these areas. There were other sects whose practices were very much alike to Cathar practices such as the groups in Cologne in Germany, and the Bogomils from what is now Bulgaria and associated regions. It has been suggested often that Catharism originated with the Bogomils and was brought to the Languedoc by Bogomil missionaries. While this is indeed a possibility there are subtle differences between the two groups which suggests perhaps another, more home-grown and indigenous dualist

tradition was already there. I suggest that perhaps the Cathars had a Priscillianist root system which in its turn, like many similar so called 'heresies could trace themselves back to the Essenes of Jerusalem among whose members most likely was counted Jesus and most of his followers. Whatever the reason for their being, by 1143, the majority of Christians in the region were Cathar. Bernard of Clairveaux campaigned in the region against their practices but had no success whatsoever. Increasingly, the Popes became alarmed.

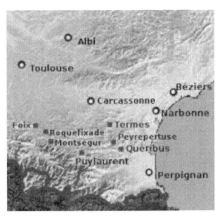

Like the followers of Priscillian the Cathars had two levels of believer: most were the ordinary people who were allowed, though not encouraged, to marry - although strictly as a bond and not a sacrament -

and bring up their families. These were the *credentes*. They were craftsmen and women, hardworking weavers, metalworkers and potters. Above them were the *Perfecti*. It is hard for us to image the status these men and women had. Like their counterparts amongst the Essenes, these were the Pure Ones, those who had achieved perfection and redemption in this life. These *Parfaits* and *Parfaites* had renounced the earthly realm by receiving the only sacrament valid for the Cathars: the Consolamentum. To call this a baptism would be highly misleading. The Cathars renounced baptism as being of the material world. The Consolamentum meant baptism with the spirit and through it the supplicant received the Holy Paraclete, the gift of the Holy Spirit in exactly the same way that Christ had received it at the time of his baptism. For the Cathars the water was not only unnecessary but tainted. This was more a symbolic baptism of fire after which the *Parfait* became a comforter and a preacher of the only true way to the resurrection they had received, in this life. This is in many ways the core of the Gnostic beliefs and there is little doubt that both Cathars and Priscillianists were Gnostics especially when this realisation of the truth is linked to their dualism. Both groups rejected the Trinity, both made the extraordinary claim that redemption flowed from the understanding of the true nature of man's being, as pure spirit trapped in matter through either curiosity, or the machinations of a devilish trickster who wanted us to believe that faith in Jesus' death on the cross was all we needed to know for our salvation after death.

Following Jesus' perhaps most difficult exhortation, the Cathar perfect once they had received the Consolamentum, were expected to leave their wives, husbands, families. They lived together in houses. When death was close, rather than submit themselves to the decay of the flesh, they would starve themselves to death in fast called the *Endura*. Not surprisingly, most *credentes* waited until their deathbed before asking to receive the Consolamentum. In the Roman Catholic Church, the rite of Extreme Unction was introduced at about this time to compete with the deathbed ritual of the Cathars.

The Cathars had no doubt that the world and the association with the world was linked with Satan. Jesus could not have died on the cross as what perished was the body, not the spirit. The true world, they said, was spiritual, eternal and immaterial, in fact the antithesis of matter. The world eternal was the spiritual renewal of the elected day by day, the knowledge of Christ's kingdom and never of this world. Satan was the king of the world, the visible, temporal world of the named and thus the desired. As Jehovah in the Old Testament, he had showed his true colours by pretending to be, or perhaps even believing that he was God, the Creator of all. Satan for the Cathari was the lord of the physical person, the decaying flesh which lusts and covets and makes people sin. Simply put, for the Cathars - and Priscillian - we are not meant to be here. Humans are the production of the fall of certain angels who followed Samael the Blind One in his fall to earth and were persuaded by him to enter into the bodies of the creatures he made out of sand and dust. When the angels realised the trick that had been played upon them, they longed to escape from their material bodies to return to their celestial selves of pure spirit from which they were taken by false promises and to which they hoped one day to return. The aim of life for the Cathars, then, was to reverse the fall: to re-unite the spirit with the body and in so-doing free oneself from the imprisonment of the soul.

So what, then, is the world? Simply put: hell. This, folks is the realm of the Devil - you are in the Matrix, trapped on the island like Truman and the only way you are going to break out is to come to the realisation of what you are, where you have come from, what binds you to this world of suffering, and what you have to do to extricate your soul. And you'd better wake up soon or you are destined to continue to be trapped in ignorance for many lifetimes. Some very notable comparisons between the Cathars and the Priscillianists can be made here: both groups were vegetarians eating no meat or meat products, although fish appears to have been allowed since fish, according to the Cathars, did not have sexual intercourse to reproduce. Neither group drank wine as it was considered not only intoxicating to the spirit but contaminated with the earth of the material world. I am not sure what they thought about leeks and carrots. But I digress. Both groups were expected to pray, day and night, but while Priscillian asked his followers to read all books including the Apocrypha it seems more likely that such books were not available to the Cathari who seemed to take much of their doctrine from the Gospel of St. John. This is not to say however, that there could not have been an oral tradition of additional material or perhaps they may even have had one or more of the so-called heretical writings as part of the much-written about "Cathar treasure". The Cathars had no respect for the cross likening it to "the gallows on which your father was hanged". Instead their symbol was the dove of peace. Scorning the open and visible opulence in which the clergy and particularly the Pope lived, they sought voluntary poverty. They denied the Apostolic Succession believing the Catholic Popes to be the Antichrist. The *Perfecti* aimed to live their lives in purity. Once they had taken the Consolamentum they became quite

 literally Christs themselves, and it is for this reason that the *credentes* would worship them, often by prostration, not because of any attempt at worldly glorification on their part but because they beheld the living God.

The Synod of Verona took place in 1184. It was convened for the specific purpose of condemning the Waldensians, another Gnostic group whose beliefs were very similar to those of the Cathars who also travelled and preached in pairs as did the Bogomils. It was clearly only a matter of time. In 1198, the very mis-named Innocent III tried to launch a crusade against the Cathars but couldn't drum up much support. The nobles and knights lived side by side with the Cathars, some, such as the Count of Toulouse, were clearly Cathar sympathisers and in some cases, their mothers and sisters were *Parfaits* and *Parfaites*. "Why would we want to persecute them?" the knights said in Albi. "They are our neighbours and our friends and we respect them and their honest work". Innocent had to be content with seething and fuming while his church became more and more shipwrecked by the doubts of the people. But after Cathar sympathisers were suspected in the murder of a Papal legate near Toulouse in 1109, Innocent decided to make a call for Holy War and this time he had the backing of the

King of France. He exhorted the knights to exercise their religious zeal, promising them full remission of sins for any deeds they carried out in the name of God. These men, for the most part, were mercenaries interested in nothing but the spoils of war. Near Beziers, a town of some 20,000 both Cathar and Catholic, the townspeople were so terrified of the massed forces that they hid in the Church of Mary Magdalene. When asked by a commander what he should do in this situation, their leader Armaud Amaury most famously exclaimed: "Kill them all; God will recognise his own".

What followed over the next 40 years was some of the most blatant butchery ever  carried out in the name of Jesus. At Minerve after a long and drawn out siege which ended when the water supply was contaminated, 140 went to the flames. When the knights approached their leader - who had offered clemency to any who accepted the Catholic faith - and said that they weren't there to see heretics escape, he told them not to worry. "They won't recant", he said. He was right. Chroniclers of the time say that the heretics "hurled themselves into the flames". At Lavaur, 400 Perfecti died the same death. Finally in 1244 at Montsegur, perhaps the most famous Cathar site of all, 225 *Parfaits* and *Parfaites* died by being burned alive at the bottom of the mountain upon which stood the castle which had been the last remaining Cathar stronghold.

I'd like to deviate for just a quick minute here to tell a story and suggest a question. After a prolonged siege, the defences of the castle of Montsegur were breached by a group of Gastons. The residents asked for 15 days to prepare for their deaths and distributed their clothes and few possessions to prepare for a death they did not believe in. Those who were *credentes* were given the option of deciding during those days whether they would give up their faith and walk free or not. It is on record that 20 *credentes* asked the leading Parfait Bertrand Marti to be consoled.

What is extraordinary about this is that as ordinary believers they could have survived the capitulation, but as *Parfaits* they knew they would be burned alive. The words of the Consolamentum are known to us. Part of the sacrament states that the supplicant says: "I have this will and determination. Pray to God for me that he will give me strength". They would have needed it.

I have been to Montsegur. I left a white rose on a rock. To this day the atmosphere is redolent of sadness, injustice, and ignorance. I felt no glory there.

After this, there appeared to be no more organised Cathar resistance although the practice continued in secret, much as it is likely the Priscillianists had to take their conventicles out from the houses of adherents and elite to clearings in the forest, mountain retreats etc. But the Popes knew that the threat remained. By 1226, the second crusade against heresy had crushed the southern counts and the entire region had been annexed to France under the Capetian rule of St. Louis who had headed the Crusade in person. Meanwhile, in 1229, a Spanish priest named Dominic, a religious fanatic and thoroughly unpleasant man, although it must be said that he cannot be held directly responsible for the deeds of the Dominican Inquisition which he founded as by then he was already dead.

For several years, now, I have spoken words of peace to you. I have preached to you; I have besought you with tears. But as the common saying goes in Spain: where a blessing fails a good thick stick will succeed. Now we shall rouse princes and prelates against you; and they, alas, will in their turn assemble whole nations and peoples and a mighty number will perish by the sword. Towers will fall and walls will be razed to the ground. And you will all of you be reduced to servitude. Thus force will prevail where gentle persuasion has failed to do so.

 These are the words of Christian "Saint" Dominic to the Christian "heretic": the Cathars. The Lamb to the Wolves... The Inquisition was charged to do anything at all they wished to force Cathars to recant. This stopped short of actual torture or death. They then handed over their victims to the secular forces for that. Any and every means could and was used to exact the "truth" from these poor innocent men and women in order to save them from eternal damnation, the perpetrators never knowing that it was they

themselves who already lived in hell. The atmosphere of distrust in towns and villages grew daily. Anyone could be arrested on the grounds that they carried on heretical practices, never knowing the exact nature of their so-called crimes, not the identity of their accusers. Bodies of suspected heretics were dug up to be thrown to the flames. By the middle of the 14th century, there was not a Cathar left.

So, I suppose that brings me back to me.

If God is all good

If God is All Powerful

If God is all knowing

Why do evil things happen?

The problem is, as has been pointed out by the Rev. Doctor Stephen Hoeller of the Los Angeles Gnostic Church, that it is impossible to reconcile these premises one with another. Personally, I think I may have predated Dr. Hoeller since I figured this out at the age of 16 around about the time I dropped God. If God is all good but allows catastrophe and evil to exist then he is not all powerful. If he is all powerful and allows such things to happen, then he is not all good at all.Ah, but I hear you say: Evil came about because of man's original sin and we have been paying for it ever since. The sins of the fathers and all that. According to Saint Augustine, who turned tailcoat against the Manichees the minute he realised what had happened to Priscillian could happen to him, "sin" as a sexually transmitted disease.

What rubbish! Jesus would turn in his grave.

Let's take the proposition that God created man in his own image. This begs the question: "What image?" If we are speaking of a physical image, well all well and good. But if that is so then God must suffer the same decay as we do, and the same bodily inconveniences which I will leave to your imagination. If, however, we posit that this may have meant "in God's intellectual image" (the *Nous*), then we have to assume that not only does man have free will, but the right to use it. That being so, it is hardly surprising that Adam would have found Eve's gift of interest. And what if man was not exactly created, but partook of the spiritual image of God? Then surely that would make man Godlike, or perhaps even God as a piece of a hologram is the whole hologram. Even though holograms didn't exist when I was sixteen, this was the form my reasoning was taking. Is it possible, I thought, that God might not be the good, powerful, knowing being that we have been told to worship? Suppose, having created man, God found out that his creation somehow was smarter than he had expected him to be? Or conversely, is it possible that God thought man his creation simple and foolish and unlikely to give Him any trouble? It all boils down to the rather more plausible possibility that either man was intended to be an automaton, created to serve a lesser God who being All Good should not have debased his creation in such a way, or else, man proved to be too smart for God to handle hence the prohibitions about trees and apples and all. Man, he found, was investigative: he, and she, seeks knowledge as a way to truth, and having found the means to that truth becomes all knowledgeable, all powerful, and good. What is the nature of that truth? Could it be that man and woman, realising their bondage to their earthly bodies, recognised that within them was a heavenly spirit, forever at one with and a part of the true God? Could it be that this investigation led Eve and Adam to the conclusion that the one they have been told to worship "above all others" is not only jealous, but deeply flawed! What would be the one and only outcome of this conclusion? Atheism: apostasy before religion had even been created. Now obviously "God" couldn't have that and so to punish Adam, Eve and all humankind to come for daring to challenge his orders, they would be forever removed from this paradise he had created for them where they had been expected to remain forever in ignorance of their true origins. Such reasoning only led me to the conclusion that either:

God is not all good - because he either denied his creation access to their true natures, or else put temptation deliberately in their way so that he could exercise his power over them whether they transgressed or not. A God who wishes to keep his creations in the cave of ignorance cannot be all good.

God is not all knowing or else he would have realised that his creature was no fool. "God" is blind to the true nature of his creation, and blind to the fact that he is neither good nor powerful. His name is Samael, the Blind One, and he is evil personified.

God is not all powerful - he could have prevented them from having the longing for knowledge had he wanted to.

Strong words?

Consider these then:

slavery, genocide, terrorism, poverty, environmental catastrophe, paedophilia, sex slavery, ignorance, squalor, domestic violence, rape, the exploitation of the weak majority by the rich minority, and the inability to free our minds from religious institutions which in order to secure our loyalty must keep us in state of perpetual fear!

If man is responsible for all this, how can he have been created in the image of a Perfect God: perfection cannot admit evil or it is not perfection. If God is responsible for this, well, he has one hell of a lot to answer for!

Who created evil? Satan? Perhaps. But who is Satan? Is he the same as the Devil and how did he get to have such a hold over us? There is only one conclusion, that which we have been taught to worship as God, even knowing or perhaps despite the horrors of the Old Testament and the evidence of our own television screens, is not God. This god is deeply flawed, malicious and insecure, ignorant of his own weaknesses and caprices, jealous of...?

In fact, God is indeed all good etc., but there is another God who perfectly fits this description. And once we realise this, the heaviness of the world, the imperfections of our bodies, the torment of our minds as they strive to make a sense of this life we have been thrown into, all assume their proper place as subservient to our true nature and are allowed to return to our true home, not as the Catholic church will tell you, after death, but in this life. We can be resurrected in the flesh as pure spirit.

> *Master, when shall the kingdom come? And he answered us straightways: It will not come by waiting for it. It will not be a matter of saying, Here it is or There it is. Rather the kingdom of the Father is spread upon the earth. But men do not see it.*

You will not find this is the New Testament; you will not even find it exactly as it is written here in the Gnostic Writings. It is an excerpt from The *Apocryphon of Jesus the Christ* which Kieran in

Pilgrimage to Heresy is translating. As far as I know, no such gospel exists, yet the words are pure Gnostic, pure Priscillian, pure Cathar, and they are what I have come to believe in myself.

> *The world came about by a mistake. For he who created it wanted to make it imperishable and immortal. But he fell short of attaining his desire. For the world never was immortal, nor for that matter was he who made the world.*

Who would ever have thought to find Jesus saying these words? Yet in the Gnostic writings they are repeated many times.

The disciples asked Jesus: Lord, when will the New World come? And he answered them: What you look forward to has already come and you still do not realise it.

The disciples entreated him: Lord, how shall we know truth from falsehood?

The saviour answered us thus: woe to those who are captives. For they are bound in caverns. In mad laughter do they rejoice in what they think you see. They neither realise their perdition, nor do they reflect upon their circumstances. They do not realise that they have dwelt in darkness and death.

Some will say the lord died first and rose up, they are in error for he will rise up first and then die. If you do not attain the resurrection first then you too will die.

"First there is a mountain, then there is no mountain, then there is."

And so back to "why do I like Gnosticism"?

Did the belief leave with the last to die? I don't know. What I do know is that there is a hunger in the world today. A hunger to release us from the chains of econotheism, and the wholesale worship of technology: of the Easy Option. Perhaps it is a hunger of the developed world which ignores or pays mere lip service to the real hunger of countries like Eritrea, Haiti, Pakistan... But whatever it is, it has a hold on many of us. Perhaps you recognise yourself here: wondering just what it is that you were put on this earth to do, or the even more difficult question: in terms of science, does my life count for nothing? Will I make no real mark on the grand scale of the existence (chaotic existence or...?) of this planet? Am I just a spread of time being birth and death? Am I a "waste of space"?

Why do I like Gnosticism? I am going to try: I like Gnosticism because it respects me as a person, a spirit, a flight of occasional fancy, an intellect, a once-in-a-while penitent, a craving, a light, a dreamer, a child in the clearing. I like Gnosticism because it respects my questioning mind; it does not seek to chain me to irreconcilable paradox to which I am told I must believe because it is absurd.

I like Gnosticism because it gives me liberation from the world, resurrection of the body, restitution of the Spirit in this life. It allows me to see the beauty of the world but not the need to identify with it in order to find my true home. *"It restoreth my soul"*

I like Gnosticism.

I hope you do too.

* See "Being and Paradox: A New Look at Anthropocentricism" for a better understanding of how this can be a world view.

If any of these persons or times have sparked your interest, I recommend the following novels in the Camino Chronicles series. See the following pages for extracts. All are available on Kindle and Softcover.

Priscillian: Pilgrimage to Heresy: Don't Believe Everything They Tell You

The first archbishop: St. James' Rooster: A Book for Pilgrims and Kingmakers

The Cathars and Montsegur: Wellspring: The Grail, The Reich, and the Man in the Black Hat

https://www.goodreads.com/book/show/7214722-pilgrimage-to-heresy

and more. Se the following pages for extracts of the historical part of each.

Extract 1: Pilgrimage to Heresy: Don't Believe Everything They Tell You

A small procession accompanied Delphidius' last journey. We walked the short distance to the grain field. The small green shoots were already well above the ground and the poppies grew all around the circumference. I had expected to see Priscillian and the other two bishops in their episcopal robes, but Salvianus and Instantius were dressed in simple togas, while Priscillian's robe was plainer still: a white linen tunic, unbound at the waist and with no fastenings that I could see. It looked to be made without seams. I had chosen a pale green silk - Delphidius' favourite. It was unadorned. Procula was in blue. The rest, I forget.

Marcellus the farmer was waiting for us. He too was dressed in a very simple white robe.

Priscillian took the Urn from me.

"Your husband was the greatest of men; yet he has chosen the simplest of ends. His desire was to return to the earth of the place where he was born. To grow once more in his own fields."

We had formed a line at the edge of the newly burgeoning crops. The sun behind us had scattered its light into strata: aqua blue, apple green, the softest pinks and peaches. The birds ceased their singing. A sliver of orange rose on the horizon ahead. Priscillian and the farmer walked forwards into the field. We remained. Not a word was spoken by anyone. The sliver gradually turned into a fireball. Priscillian handed the urn to Marcellus, and then slipped out of his sandals. Then, to my astonishment, he pulled his robe over his head. He was naked. He took the urn once more and walked forward again. He raised it to the ascending moon. He seemed to be speaking but the words were lost to me, they seemed to be in another language - Greek perhaps - and besides, at that moment a small breeze came up and carried them away. He continued to walk forward, scattering my husband's ashes into his own fields. Covering the life of the green shoots with a layer of grey.

It took me then. The tears I had held back coursed down my cheeks. I felt a weight on my upper chest; a strangled cry ceased before it began. I thought I would choke.

Priscillian was on his knees. The moon framed him like a halo. I followed him to the ground and one by one, all sank to the earth. Priscillian's voice rose in a song: I knew it not. But the two bishops joined their voices and to my utmost incredulity, so did Marcellus, the farmer, and three others of my household, one, Claudia, a dairymaid from Marcellus' farm, his daughter whom I had known from birth when I had a acted as midwife. Donatus, Marcellus's son, a young man but not unlettered thanks to my husband, raised his voice with them.

Then it was over. Salvianus and Instantius began to turn back, and we followed them. I glanced over my shoulder. Marcellus was bringing back the empty urn, but Priscillian, his robe still on the ground where it had fallen, was walking into the moon.

Extract 2: *St. James' Rooster: A book for Pilgrims and Kingmakers*

Diego Gelmirez knows how to impress. Although technically it was the chapter and clergy who were responsible for the Mass, and although, of course, Diego did not officiate since he had not been brought into Holy Orders, Diego was still a canon of the church of St. James. He also held the purse strings. The afternoon of Holy Night was technically a holiday and so I was surprised to see men working in and around the cathedral both new and old. Most were tidying up long abandoned worksites, or sweeping the paths around the old church and those leading into the new cathedral, half of which was almost complete. Some were adding wreaths of holly here and there, celebratory posies of wild grasses and mosses, apples, painted, some trimmed with ribbons and braids. As the night approached, I realised what he was doing. There were candles placed evenly along the walkway from the south door of the old church to the steps and south door of the new cathedral. After dinner, these were seen to be lit. I stepped into the transept of the new building and marvelled at what I saw.

Diego had arranged for decorations everywhere. There were tapestries covering the open scaffolding, rugs everywhere (where did he find so many?). A makeshift altar had also been procured and was covered with cloth of gold and silver candleholders. The total effect was nothing other than magical. Like stepping into a dream.

"Do you like it?" Diego had followed me in.

"It is truly a transformation! Most impressive."

"I hope you will not be the only one to think so. It has been long enough now that this sacred shrine has been without a guardian and protector. The cathedral needs a bishop; Alfonso the king wants a bishop; and Duke Raymond believes he knows the man for the job."

"You?" It was not really a question on my part. I knew Diego, and although he had been heard to say that he did not envy the one chosen for the job I knew he had been working to this end for many years now.

"And why not? Who knows more about this town than I do? Who knows the people better? Though I have my detractors, they are not the ones who count. By and large, the nobles know me well, and love me well."

"And what do you know of God, Diego?"

It was a bold question, but by now I knew him well enough to venture it. And I knew him well enough to have an answer.

"God wants His Holy Apostle protected. He wants his shrine to be visited by countless pilgrims and venerated by kings. God wants Compostela and its cathedral to be glorified forever in the hearts and minds of all the people all over Christendom and beyond into the heathen lands. And God has told me that if I can ready my own heart to receive His guidance, then it will come to me in full measure."

"But, forgive me; you are not a pious man, Diego. You keep the Lord's Day as well as any, but the other six you are more involved in silver than saving souls."

I wondered if I had gone too far. But Diego only laughed.

"You, too, know me well, Pedro. But pious men have almost broken this church in two. And even he who began to put it back together again did not know enough of the times to be on the right side. Only Dalmatius in recent years understood what this cathedral could stand for. And he learned it from his master Hugh of Cluny, a man I hope to have the pleasure of meeting in person in the not too distant future. Compostela must have a new bishop, Pedro, and destiny says that that man will be the one who stands before you. It must be. I shall go to Rome with Duke Raymond's approbation and God's blessing. I think it is time I made a pilgrimage."

Just then the bells began, calling us to mass.

"I must go now, Pedro. I wish you make merry at Christmas, and by the way, I believe you may have need of two horses tomorrow...?"

"How did you know that?" I said, astonished. I hadn't even asked him yet.

"Don't think you are the only one here who knows everything. And now I really must go..."

And as he went I heard him mutter: "And when I am bishop, I really must do something about those bells."

Extract 3: Wellspring: The Grail, The Reich, and The Man in the Black Hat

The moon was high in the sky by the time we had all gathered together. My father and my husband stood side by side on a large trestle which was usually used by our Bishop Bertrand for our services and celebrations. Pèire stood with his hands behind his back. A gesture I knew well. He used it often when in company with Raymond de Pereille, perhaps a sign of acquiescence to the older man although they are equals in terms of their roles in Montsegur.

"Revered *Perfecti,* dear friends, noble knights … kindred. As you know, this morning, the Lord of Mirepoix and I went below the mountain to speak with our besiegers. It was a short journey, but probably the longest I have ever had to undertake. The king's representative, Hughes d'Arcis…."

There was muttering and mumbling from some of the men…

"….d'Arcis, and the archbishop of Narbonne were there to meet us cordially…"

"Easy to do that with ten thousand men at your back," shouted one of the men-at-arms.

"Shhh," said the others. "Let Lord Raymond finish what he has to say!"

"It has been almost nine months since the beginning. We have held out and nobly and even our persecutors allow us that. Because of this, the terms are remarkably light, lighter than I expected. Every one of you have fought in your own ways for the freedom to worship as we will, as good believers in the Cathar faith. Without our brethren the *Perfecti* and *Perfectae*, how would our souls survive the journey from here to Perfection, or another life in which to practice our holy way of being? The church of Rome knows nothing of our ways. It calls us wolves. But it is they who are the wolves; we are but humble sheep. But not so humble as to succumb to them without a good fight…"

"Sheep with sharp teeth!" shouted one wag in the assembly. Despite their weariness, the others cheered.

"These are the conditions we have negotiated, and on your behalf we have accepted:

"First of all, they have agreed to a truce lasting 15 days. No-one will enter or leave this fortress during that time. I don't have to tell you how important this period is to all of us. It is the time of *Bema*. It will give us a chance to pray, to put things in order, spend time with our families and friends, and make decisions which will decide whether we live or die. We will be exchanging hostages with them and anyone who is willing to do that will please see me in my quarters this evening after supper."

There was some low mumbling. Others remained quiet.

"Everyone who worries that their lives will be sacrificed, know this: any person who wishes will receive a full pardon provided they will recant their faith – if they are *credentes* and followers…

"What do you mean by everyone?" asked Imbert de Salas who had taken part in the massacre at Avignonet.

"As I have said, everyone who will recant and ask forgiveness will have their lives spared. Most will receive at worst a light sentence. This is what I have been informed."

Quietly, there was a noticeable shift of attention towards the *Perfecti*. They said nothing. They knew that "everyone" did not include them. They waited.

"The men-at-arms will be allowed to retire with their weapons and baggage and their families. They will be required to appear before the Inquisition to answer questions pertaining to the nature of their activities. They will also receive light penalties only."

"What do they consider a "light penalty?" asked someone. "Those bastards are not known for their clemency."

"True enough. But this is all I can tell you. At this point, that is all I know."

"What about the Count and his promises?" Once again, the speaker was Imbert.

A few weeks before, Count Raymond of Toulouse had sent a message with Matheus when he had returned up the mountain with the crossbowmen. It was a pitiful gesture on the part of the count, but better than nothing. At the time we took it as some reassurance that we were not alone. The count had asked my husband if we could hold out until Easter. Raymond sent assurance that he was building an army to march on Montsegur to raise the siege. He even claimed to be petitioning the emperor.

At first my husband was jubilant, but when no further correspondence came, and the conditions in the fortress became more and more intolerable, he had to admit that he didn't trust Raymond of Toulouse, and never had.

A few days ago we learned he is in Rome, trying to save his own soul...

"The Count's promises are like piecrusts"; said Pèire disgustedly, in answer to the question, "easily broken."

There was no response; we had long since given up hoping for a miracle.

My father continued: "All other persons in the fortress will remain at liberty, and will similarly be subject to light penalties only…" He paused assessing our faces, "provided that they abjure their 'heretical beliefs' and make confession before the Inquisitors."

"Those who will not will be burnt at the stake."

* * * * *

About Tracy Saunders

Tracy Saunders is the author of several books including The Camino Chronicles Trilogy, They Think You Are Jesus, The Indalo Quest, a travel biography, Two Girls, a children's book, and even a cookbook. She studied for her Master's degree in Philopsophy at Brock University, Canada, and later for her M.Ed. in Applied Linguistics, and her M.A, in Clinical Psychology and Clinical Hypnosis. She practised as an educational consultant at King's College, and a psychotherapist in Marbella, Spain for several years before moving to Galicia on the Camino de Santiago where she welcomes pilgrims from all over the world.

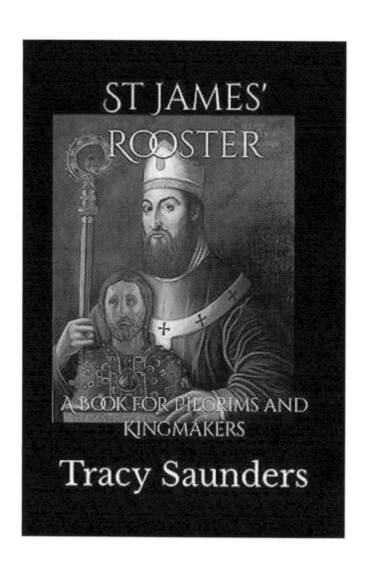

ST JAMES'
ROOSTER

A BOOK FOR PILGRIMS AND
KINGMAKERS

Tracy Saunders

WELLSPRING

THE GRAIL, THE REICH AND
THE MAN IN THE BLACK HAT

Tracy Saunders

Printed by Amazon Italia Logistica S.r.l.
Torrazza Piemonte (TO), Italy

60854752R00079